The Tap Turned on:

Poetry Flowed

DENA D. ANDREWS

AuthorHouse™
1663 Liberty Drive
Bloomington, IN 47403
www.authorhouse.com
Phone: 833-262-8899

Because of the dynamic nature of the Internet, any web addresses or links contained in this book may have changed
since publication and may no longer be valid. The views expressed in this work are solely those of the author and do not
necessarily reflect the views of the publisher, and the publisher hereby disclaims any responsibility for them.

Any people depicted in stock imagery provided by Getty Images are models,
and such images are being used for illustrative purposes only.
Certain stock imagery © Getty Images.

This book is printed on acid-free paper.

ISBN: 978-1-6655-7194-4 (sc)
ISBN: 978-1-6655-7193-7 (e)

Library of Congress Control Number: 2022917840

Print information available on the last page.

Published by AuthorHouse 10/12/2022

authorHOUSE®

Table of Contents

Abortion

Pitter-patters are those feet,
Dancing in my head.
Little hands, little feet
Curled into my side.

Making mud pies,
Hopping jump rope,
Playing hopscotch,

Mending cuts,
Untying laces,
Kissing tears away.

But those would not be my experiences,
As I shunned you
And tossed you far away.

Addiction

You are the addiction
I worked so hard to overcome.
I cannot return,
In this season of pain,
To the thing that almost broke me,
Nearly drove me insane.

You are the addiction
I worked so hard to overcome.
Robbed me of my positivity,
Stole so many nights sleep,
Took away my energy,
You plunged me into the deep.

You are the addiction
I worked so hard to overcome.
Lost my taste buds,
Dropped oh so much weight,
Down trodden and dejected,
I lost my carefree gait.

You are the addiction,
To which I cannot return.

Beauty

To be seen in one's action,
In the things we say,
The way we treat others,
The choices made each day.

It's not in the appearance,
Nor in the facade we portray,
Not the awful things we do,
Never in the unkind words we say.

True beauty defines,
Draws many near,
Like bees to honey
By the sweet aroma in the air.

Seldom seen with the eyes.

Bended Knee

The road for me seems sometimes long.
But I tarried along cause it made me strong.
No hand to hold,
Just God and me,
But I knew comfort would come,
On bended knee.

Blue

Blue, blue, blue,
The sky, the sea, the feeling you left with me.

Drifting like the clouds, flowing like the tide,
Oh how my emotions went for a ride.

Did I conjure you up or pull you from my dream?
Oh please, please tell me, what did it all mean?

Sifting through it all, it came to me.
It was merely an experiment, to see how it could be.

Hope

A new day dawns
A baby is born.
Marriages taking place,
New memories added;

Laughter returns,
Smiles observed more frequently,
Old friends reunited,
Hugs and kisses abound.

A vibrant rainbow appears on the horizon.
The sun reflects off the tranquil blue waters.
Waves caress the shoreline.
White sandy beaches beckon.

Hope is all around.

Covid

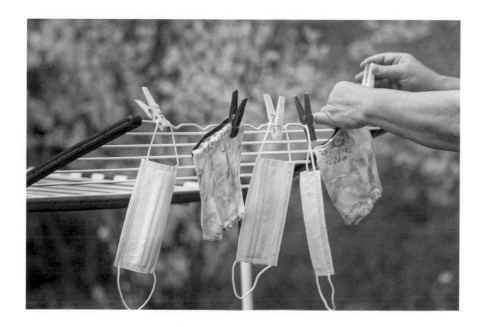

You snuck up on the world,
Set us all in disarray,
Confined us to our homes,
Admonishing us that there we'd stay.

Your deadly virus
Took many families away,
Sent many into depression,
Leaving fear that there we'd stay.

You robbed us of freely moving;
You took away our assembly;
The hugs and kisses were gone too.
The world plunged into stillness, and there we thought we'd stay.

But you taught us many lessons,
Like treasure those you love,
Make every moment count,
Live a life of purpose, and there we ought to stay.

COV-19

You knocked me out like a boxer,
Took me many a round.
When I thought I'd gained my balance,
You struck me back to the ground.

The aches in the body,
The joints' pain,
My head felt so dizzy,
I was doubtful I'd stand again.

My sore throat,
Speech like a toad,
Blurry vision to add,
Kept me off the road.

The fever was a beast;
I fought as best I could,
Lethargic and no energy,
No showers like I should.

This nasty plague
Needs to be conquered like a game,
Then sent back to the place
From whence it came.

Dancing

I feel so alive,
My heartbeat throbbing.
Every atom of my being in harmony,
Dancing, dancing, dancing.

The music pulsating,
I feel so alive.
That rhythmic motion of my body,
Dancing, dancing, dancing.

The jig, the twist, the Hully Gully,
It doesn't matter.
I feel so alive,
Dancing, dancing, dancing.

Daydream

The aroma of bacon, eggs, and cinnamon rolls
Tickle my nostrils.
A rose on my pillow,
A kiss on each eyelid,
Then my lips too.
Was that your raspy voice murmuring, "I love you"?

Did I awaken you?
Are you ready for the day?
Do you want foreplay
Or to be ravaged instead?
My body's screaming sweetie, "I love you."

Oh please, please sweetie,
I can't take it anymore.
Let me suck you and lick you
And whatever else you adore,
Ride you as I unleash the passion.
I've been wanting to tell you, "I love you."

Death

You came like a tsunami
And took them both away.
Not a moment's notice,
To say a warm goodbye.
Oh death, why did you rob me of the apples of my eye?

You destroyed our tomorrows;
You scorned at the promises;
You mocked the "I should dos";
You trampled on the hugs;
And instead, plunged me into darkness.

The days seem so much longer,
And night ne'er seems to end.
No sound is ever as joyous
As to hear them say, "Miss Veese" or "Gweeen."
Oh death, why did you rob me of the apples of my eye?

Deep Thinker

She's meticulous in her word choice,
Ponders every nuance of the chosen word,
Phrases and paraphrases to get the right context,
Deliberate in her speech,
Always a deep thinker.

She examines every conversation,
Looking for flaws in the structure,
Dissects any faux pas,
Replays each sentence,
Always a deep thinker.

She'll drive herself bananas,
Analyzing random statements,
Inferring meaning where there is none,
Coming to conclusions,
Always a deep thinker.

Did You Know

Did you mean to crash into my life this way,
Turning everything topsy-turvy as you left?

Did you not see the warning signs on my wall,
Calm and peace, a life without turmoil?

Did you not know I had common sense,
Living a life to date without any pretense?

Did you look back at the damage you had done?
What a fool I have been; because compassion, you have none.

Did you know that, like the Phoenix, still I rise?
Even though you may hear my sporadic cries.

Did you mean to offer the withered olive branch?
Too late my errant lover, I have moved on to another tranche.

Dreams

Floating on a calm sea,
Sun's rays basking down,
The light breeze caressing my skin,
Then dreams pop in.

Climbing the mountain,
Jumping in the clouds,
Breathing thin air,
Basking in Cotopaxi,

Touching the jagged walls,
Admiring the ruins,
Thinking of those brave ones
Who hewed Chichén Itzá.

Cobbled streets,
Horse drawn surreys,
Lace place settings,
Quaint architecture of Bruges.

Gazing at Tour Eiffel,
Beautiful greenery of that famous garden.
Romantically strolling Champs-Élysées,
The language caressing the ear.

Crossing Szechenyi Chain Bridge,
Staring out over the two cities,
Strolling Old Town,
Pick pockets along the street.

Thunderstorms and lightening,
I am now awake.
Eyes open and alert;
Dreams fade away.

Dying from Within

She had the operation,
Against that still small voice.
Not knowing the outcome
But more frightened
By what the tumor could be causing, dying from within.

She struggled to sit up again,
Make those steps around the home.
Eating was a challenge,
Smiling through the gloom,
While dying from within.

The last goodbye was painful,
The charge to hang in there,
A promise of relief real soon.
That final flight taken,
As you were dying from within.

Fantasy

What am I feeling?
Can you tell me?
Do you know?

You are always in my thoughts.
Is it mental stalking?
Invasion of the mind?

Do you really care?
Are you just intrigued?
Could you let me know?

Awake and alert,
Its clearer you see,
Passing time with me is just a fantasy.

Farewell

A passionate kiss,
Fondling too.
Texting quite frequently,
To say I miss you.

Gone are those days,
Of oh so much care.
Not a phone call or text,
Was his heart really there?

Bare are those memories,
Of two souls so connected.
Never needing words to express,
But oh, now I am rejected.

Oh lover of yesteryear,
"Dear John" seems a lifetime ago.
But now I'm realizing,
I was remiss in not letting you go.

Farewell.

Farewell II

Faintly tapping on my door,
You pleaded for me to give just a little more,
More of my time,
More of my heart.
But is this to be the beginning of another false start?

Words of remorse, you whispered to me,
Hoping I'd be too blinded not to see
Any change in you action,
No promise for tomorrow.
Couldn't I see I was being setup for more sorrow?

Was your heart really there?
Or was this just another fanfare?
Sex when you want it,
Sex at its best.
But dearest lover, I am not one of the saloon girls working for Mae West.

Should I cut my losses?
Move out like a pack of wild horses,
Do damage control,
Rescue my heart,
Before you again hasten your depart?

Farewell my love.
I'll say a prayer to the God above,
"Protect and keep you.
Help me to heal
From this long nightmare, which seem so surreal."

Gone

Your heart has moved on.
I do understand
Because this could never have been
Part of the Master's plan.

One woman and one man;
A family they create.
Only the devil would try
To add another mate.

I was his pawn for the moment.
A temptation I would be.
But another has stepped in
So plainly, I can see.

No rhyme or reason
Can explain
Why I succumbed to temptation,
It brings so much pain.

I'll forgive (myself) and forget.
I will move on.
For my time in your life
Now come and gone.

Goodbye

Goodbye to the errant phone call.
Goodbye to the compliment or two.
Goodbye to all the promises I hoped would come from you.

Goodbye to what could be.
Goodbye to lonely weekends.
Goodbye to all your words trying to make amends.

Goodbye to illusions.
Goodbye to pregnant dreams.
Goodbye to a torrent of tears that can fill many streams.

Goodbye melodious voice;
Goodbye to a soul full of charm.
Goodbye to your playing because it causes too much harm.

Goodbye.

Hey Pretty Girl

A child's mind
Could not process
His statements or his actions that followed.

Calling out, hey pretty girl,
What a lovely dress;
Let me touch you.

Hey pretty girl,
Let me show you something;
Then he placed his lips on mine.

Hey pretty girl,
Why are you crying?
He stroked my face with each word.

Hey pretty girl,
Come and sit on my knee.
Then he rocked back and forth as his knee invaded me.

Hey pretty girl,
It angers me to hear;
Too many painful memories conjure up my childhood fears.

I Invited You In

You were no stranger.
I called you a friend.
I let my guard down.
I invited you in.

I cooked you dinner.
I created the ambiance;
With soft lights and played jazz music.
I invited you in.

I spoke from the heart.
I apologized for my misbehavior.
I shared my spiritual journey.
I invited you in.

You switched off my music.
You tugged at my clothing.
You commanded I come closer.
I invited you in.

Your advances were unwelcomed.
My emotions were too raw.
You pushed anyway.
I invited you in.

My body is left violated.
I tremble at any touch.
I live with regret.
I invited you in.

I invited you in.

Imagine

Imagine
The hustle and bustle of pedestrian traffic,
The mad rush for the train,
Or you run down the tarmac to catch the plane.

Imagine
Chicago, Pittsburg, Minneapolis-St. Paul,
Cold winter nights with nary a star
And snow up to your ankle as you struggle to the car.

Imagine
A long walk on the beach,
The flapping of the waves as they hit the shore;
Life without adventure would be quite a bore.

Imagine.

In the Kitchen

There are fruits and vegetables,
Rice, flour, and grains;
There are poultry, fish, and meat too.
The concoction is in the making.
Don your apron,
Light the oven or the stovetop,
Let's get the cooking on!

Her directions were clear.
No need for a cookbook.
A ready palate and hungry tummy
Are all the incentives you need
To whip up that masterpiece
And release the aroma;
Let's get the cooking on!

Islands in the Sun

The jewel of the Caribbean,
America's closest neighbor in the sea,
Beautiful beaches, warm sunshine,
And horse-drawn surreys are now sporadic on our street.
But here you will also find,
The friendliest people you will ever meet.

The islands spread the archipelago.
Eco diversity abounds.
Such clear waters marveled by the astronauts
From afar.
A country with a rich heritage and
Industrious people who shoot for the star.

The culture is a mixture.
Basket weaving, boat building, wood carving
Dances of Quadrille and heel & toe;
Pieces of all those who passed through,
But anchored by the original people
And all celebrated in Junkanoo.

"We rushing,
We rushing"
The chants of Junkanoo
And Goombay summer fun
Celebrated by all
Of our islands in the sun!

Junkanoo

The horns blasting that sweet music,
The pounding on the goat skin drums,
The dancers gyrate in harmony,
Those colorful costumes,
The people uniting
All spell our sweet Junkanoo.

Throngs of people on Bay Street,
Patrons sitting or standing,
The morning draft unruffled us,
Police, judges, and marshals go by,
But we will not move
As we await our sweet Junkanoo.

The streets come alive!
As we hear the cowbells shake,
Loud chants of "who in the morning?"
The horn blowers render the entry chorus,
The drummers take the cue,
And these all herald the arrival of our sweet Junkanoo.

Listen

Listen when they don't answer.
Listen when the question is dodged.
Listen when they drift away in conversation.
Listen when they are too busy to converse.
Listen.

Listen when they recount their callousness.
Listen when they take no action.
Listen when they utter wrong timing.
Listen when "work" is always the excuse.
Listen.

So much said in the unspoken words.
So much told by what's left undone.
So much read in body language.
So much learned by what's a priority.
Listen.

Maasai Mara

What excellence,
What allure,
Greeted me on my arrival to Sarova Mara.
The entrance image of the Maasai sets the stage,
For an experience of the page.

Transported in time,
To nature so untouched,
The animals roamed,
Wastelands undisturbed,
There are also sightings of many birds.

I placed my order
Of the animals, I wished to see.
The big five
Was a must
Anything else would be unjust.

Lion,
Elephant,
Rhino,
Buffalo
And the leopard, are the big five.

The sounds of the wild,
The smell of the earth,
Images never seen
As in the beginning of time;
It was truly divine.

Animals roaming freely,
I will never compare,
To caged animals
Kept in a zoo;
Although sometimes it's the best we can do.

The oneness with nature,
It seemed unreal,
With danger all around,
Yet seeming so normal;
You knew to discard anything formal.

The beauty was phenomenal!
The air seemed heavy.
The Maasai were so intriguing.
The lessons abound;
Like an invitation to stay around.

My Ocean

If the Caribbean is a paradise,
What is its treasured jewel?
Is it the bountiful deposit of sunshine
Or the sandy white beaches?
Is it a climate bordering on perfection?
Or is it the wonderful people you meet?

The food here is to die for
The fruits entice you to have some more.
The pace of life slows down,
Thereby enabling you
To be enchanted by its richest jewel.
It is my ocean.

Mystery Man

He is dark and handsome.
He has a calm demeanor,
A gentle manner,
A good conversationalist,
He always makes me laugh,
But he's a mystery man.

He carries his dark secrets.
Seeks out the calm,
Staring out at the ocean,
Treasuring time alone,
Connects with his master,
But he's a mystery man.

One day he will open up.
Share those hidden pains,
Laugh with the same unreservedness
He evokes in others.
Smile from the eyes.
He will leave behind the mystery man.

New Morning

A new morning's broken,
The star's gone from the sky.
The sunlight peeks in.
Faint humming in the background,
As life begins to stir again.

The day presents promise;
Of all things new.
Opportunities laid out
To be embraced or rejected
As demonstrated in the things we chose to do.

A new morning's broken,
The possibilities are unlimited.
Step forth with purpose,
Pick up your charge
As life begins to stir again.

Oh, My Bahamas

I did not feel the raindrops on my face.
Although I was hoarse from screaming,
my throat felt no pain.
There was no ache in my legs from jumping up and down.
My pulsating heart and the joy within
Overtook the moment.
The proponents of corruption were defeated.
A new day had dawned for The Bahamas.
Sunshine overcast the islands.
A new hope formed.
I was proudly able to say oh, my Bahamas.

One Tear

The sun's gone in,
No star to brighten the sky.
Is this truly happening?
Or has my whole life been a lie?

Days of endless joy,
Gone faint in nigh one night,
Or was I searching for something,
That was never really in sight.

Your words of so much passion,
The beginning of my plight,
For oh, too soon would come,
The long and lonely night.

Too long, I stood here waiting,
Often wishing I could die.
But as I struggle with emotions,
Only a tear fell from my eye.

Otavalo Market

Teeming with tourists,
Bartering on every side;
There are rugs, artwork, jewelry, and accessories.
The items litter Otavalo's market
The artisans beam with pride.

The sellers' eyes glisten as tourists fondle their wares.
They are immediately excited at the prospect of a sale.
Their chorus of "tourist dollar, tourist dollar"
As they urge you to spend.
Trying every trick of their trade
Hoping you bend.

Poinciana

Majestic is your trunk,
Radiant is your orange flowers,
Bean pods filled with music,
Poignant is your aroma,
Oh, beautiful Poinciana
Bloom more for me each day.

Some dislike the petals that you drop,
Throughout your summer stay,
Creating flowerbeds along the highway,
But they are the route's most pleasant view.
Oh, beautiful Poinciana,
Bloom more for me each day.

Raindrops

Drip drip,
Are those drops
That falls on the roof.

That pitter-patter,
Faintly tapping,
Echoes in the room.

The grass stands up,
The flowers smile,
The earth embraces her.

Raindrops, raindrops
Falling gently down,
They splatter to the ground.

She Said No

Hair pulled in one
Revealing her beautiful jawline;
Red lips and pink cheeks,
She is a lovely vision to behold.

Cutoff top
Exposing her midriff;
Tight jeans showing her curves
Stiletto pumps to add.

Her walk
A seductive gait;
Hips swaying,
An entrance she made.

Eyes riveted upon her.
They follow her every move.
Her confidence exudes.
Her presence charms.

Men clamoring for her attention,
She selectively bestows.
Despite the outward appearance,
Her chastity she holds dear.

They say she is a tease,
Needed a lesson to be taught;
Tearing at her clothing,
They groped her body.

She screamed for help.
All observers turned away;
Letting her assaulters have their play.
Despite her screams, no.

Silence

No human voices,
Audio was turned off,
No birds chirping,
No automobiles traversing the street,
No airplanes taking off.

At that moment there's silence.

Mind at rest
Absolutely nothing to do,
The creaking of the wood in the roofing,
The faintest humming of appliances,
The wind whistled through the trees.

Those are the nearest sounds to be heard
Invading that moment when there's silence.

Spotty Clouds

Ever wondered,
Why the sky looked spotted?
Why the blue peeked faintly through?
Why the white clouds seemed intermeshed,
And asked is Jesus watching you?

Ever wondered,
Why the air seemed still?
And the birds' chirping gone away,
Why the silence seems deafening,
And asked is Jesus watching you?

Ever wondered,
Why time seemed to stand still?
No pressing errand to run,
And no phone calls come through
And asked is Jesus watching you?

Ever wondered,
Why the night dragged on?
No friendly face popped in,
Thoughts a far away,
And asked is Jesus watching you?

Ever wondered

Summer

Twas a balmy day,
Sweat beads on the brow,
The air was still,
Nothing moved.

The leaves wilted,
Insects sought the flower's nectar,
People stayed inside,
The sun scorched.

The air conditioners hummed.
Homes without flung their windows open,
Chilled lemonade abounds.
Summer is here.

The Twinkle is Gone

The twinkle's gone from my eye.
I try each day to find the reason,
Reason to go on,
The morning turns to night,
And still no purpose in sight,
This hurt is immeasurable.
The twinkle's gone from my eye.

I knew when I'd lost you,
My heart skipped many beats,
A void consumed me,
The panic set in,
Loneliness overtook me.
The twinkle's gone from my eye.

Tomorrow's so uncertain,
You both are no longer here,
Why oh, why did you leave me?
No journey will e'er be complete.
The experiences will be so different,
The twinkle's gone from my eye.

The Untamed Spirit

A constant thirst for exploration,
The parts yet unknown,
Whether they be within or shores afar.

The hunger to know,
Will never be quenched,
As the world keeps turning and another door stands ajar.

Thread on wandering spirit,
So much to learn,
The journey to discovery keeps you targeting that shooting star.

Tranquility

Waves gently caressing the shoreline,
Children frolicking in the sand,
Caribbean music faintly playing,
Seagulls gliding by;
Such tranquility,
Found sitting here in the shade.

That salty smell of the ocean,
The murmur of conversations,
Staring out to the horizon,
White clouds gently hover;
Such tranquility,
Found sitting here in the shade.

Then the wave crashes
Onto the rocks,
Children's shrieks are heard.
A leisure boat kicks up wake.
Tranquility no longer,
Found sitting here in the shade

Was That You

Was that you?

Sending electrodes beaming across the room?
Emitting that magnetic pull to my body,
With robotic motion, I came to you.

Was that you?

Tantalizing my daily thoughts,
Riding on my dream waves,
Nudging me awake?

Was that you?

Gently stroking my forearm?
Whispering in my ear?
Dropping butterfly kisses on my cheek?

Was that you?

Darling
Yes, yes to all your questions
My body yearns to answer.

It is me.

Watch Your Tone

Watch your tone.
Who is your audience?
Does it matter?

Watch your tone.

Watch your tone.
Do you need help?
Can you do it yourself?

Watch your tone.

Watch your tone.
Do you care about the outcome?
How will it impact you?

Watch your one.

What If?

What if we never got to speak again?
What if you never get to see my smile again?
What if the smell of my perfume never
invaded your nostrils again?
What if you never felt my touch on your skin again?
What if there are no more tomorrows
for you and me to share?
What If?

Water

It must be watered.
The grass,
The plants,
The fruit trees,
The earth,
You and me too

It's 80% percent of our bodies.
A sprinkle sustains nothing.
Parched lips, organ dysfunction,
Everything would eventually wither
Wither up and die.
You and me too

What about relationships?
A connection of human bodies,
Watering needed there too.
Starve it of water,
It withers up and dies.
You and me too

You are Here

At my lowest point
I always knew you were there;
Guiding me,
Protecting me,
Carrying me to a safe harbor
As the waves of emotions threatened to consume me.

The darkness around me
Appeared to encamp me;
But you were there
Guiding me,
Protecting me,
Carrying mc to a safe harbor
As the waves of emotions threatened to consume me.

The tears blinded me.
The pain choked me;
But I knew you were there
Guiding me,
Protecting me,
Carrying me to safe harbor,
As the waves of emotions threatened to consume me.

As I step from the ashes
I begin to see Your light again;
Guiding me,
Protecting me,
Carrying me to a safe harbor
As the waves of emotions threaten to consume me.

You are here.

Printed in the United States
by Baker & Taylor Publisher Services